With Christ
His Passion

1. Elizabeth Prout

With Christ in His Passion

Elizabeth Prout (1820–1864),
Foundress of the
Sisters of the Cross and Passion
of Our Lord Jesus Christ

Sister Dominic Savio Hamer CP

GRACEWING

First published in 2008

Gracewing
2 Southern Avenue, Leominster
Herefordshire HR6 0QF

ISBN 978 0 85244 183 1

Typesetting by
Action Publishing Technology Ltd, Gloucester, GL1 5SR

Contents

Illustrations

2. 29/31 Byrom Street, Deansgate, Manchester

3. Chapel behind 31 Byrom Street

Introduction

On 9 April 1875 a Passionist priest, Father Alphonsus
O'Neill, presided over a very special ceremony in the convent
of the Sisters of the Cross and Passion of Our Lord Jesus
Christ at 31 Byrom Street, Manchester. In preparation, a new
chapel had been built at the rear of the convent. It had been
officially opened on the previous 21 November with a High
Mass in the presence of a large number of clergy and benefactors. Pointed Gothic in style, it was built of grey stock
brick with stone dressings. The interior walls were lined with
rich pine skirtings and the flooring of the aisles was inlaid
with mosaic tiles. The roof, formed of pointed principals
springing from stone corbels, showed six bays each holding a
rich, silvery plate of stained glass, bearing the Passionist Sign
or Badge, emblems of Christ's Passion and the Scriptural
text, *Christ was made obedient unto death, even to the death
of the Cross.* Four days later, on 25 November 1874, the
parishioners of St Mary's, Mulberry Street, had crowded into
the new chapel for Benediction and a sermon given by Father
Alphonsus O'Neill. Then, on Friday, 9 April 1875, Father
Alphonsus returned. He came on behalf of the Passionist
Father General, Father Dominic Giacchini, to present each
Professed Sister with the Passionist Sign. Henceforth, each
one would wear it over her heart to distinguish her as a
member of the Congregation of the Sisters of the Cross and
Passion, aggregated to the Congregation of the Passion
founded by St Paul of the Cross. In his sermon at the opening

4. Fr Alphonsus O'Neill CP

of the new chapel, Father Alphonsus had reviewed the Sisters' history since the foundation of the Congregation at 69 Stocks Street, Cheetham Hill, Manchester in 1851. He had noted its rapid increase in numbers and its expansion in the dioceses of Salford and Liverpool. It was this last ceremony in April 1875, however, that marked the culmination of the founding process begun in poverty, ridicule and sectarian tension almost a quarter of a century earlier, for it was the conferring of the Passionist Sign that fulfilled the dreams of the Foundress, Elizabeth Prout.

Chapter One

Childhood and Youth

Elizabeth Prout was born on 2 September 1820 in the ancient English town of Shrewsbury, close to the Welsh border. Her father, Edward Prout, had been born in London about 1795 and had been baptized a Catholic. Although Catholics in England had been allowed freedom of worship since 1778, there were very few churches or priests, whilst a new era of anti-Catholicism had been inaugurated by Lord George Gordon in the riots he provoked in 1780. Many English Catholics continued to remain true to their faith, as their families had during more than two centuries of persecution. Many others, however, had lapsed, either from lack of opportunity to attend Mass and receive the sacraments, or because they were pressurized by renewed opposition. Whatever the reason in his case, Edward Prout had already stopped practising his Catholic faith before he married Ann Yates in All Saints' Anglican parish church in Wellington, Shropshire on 5 February 1820. His wife, on the other hand, was a staunch member of the Church of England. Accordingly when Elizabeth, their first and only child, was born a delicate and apparently premature baby, Ann Prout took care to have her baptized when only a fortnight old, on 17 September 1820, in St Julian's Anglican church, Shrewsbury.

Edward Prout was a journeyman cooper, working in the Coleham Brewery in Shrewsbury's industrial suburb on the outer side of the River Severn and across from the Catholic chapel high on the town walls. There an ironworks beside the brewery, so that Elizabeth lived in an industrial, working-class environment. Whenever she crossed the river into old Shrewsbury, however, she stepped into a different civilization. The old Grey Friars' house, the castle, the Benedictine abbey, St Mary's with its treasury of medieval stained glass and the black and white timbered buildings along the narrow streets were all part of her culture. When she was only six years old, however, the owners of the Salopian Brewery found themselves in financial difficulties. The brewery was put up for sale. When no other brewers showed an interest, it was bought in 1831 by the owner of the ironworks for storing timber. Edward Prout had to seek another job.

On national census night, 1841, Edward Prout, his wife, Ann, their daughter, Elizabeth, his mother-in-law, Mary Yates and a little boy, Charles Tafft, were living in New Brewery Yard, Stone, Staffordshire. Their house belonged to Joule's Brewery and was across from the cooperage, where Edward Prout worked. Stone was different from Shrewsbury. Although it had some timbered buildings, Elizabeth Prout's Stone centred on the red brick of the brewery buildings. St Michael's Anglican church, however, which she and her mother probably attended on Sundays, was a stately edifice, built about 1770 on the site of an Augustinian priory, so that the town was not without its medieval connections.

As an artisan's daughter, Elizabeth received a basic English education. Apart from her religion and her education, her upper working-class home was the most formative influence in her life. Her father was a skilled craftsman. He was a man with a trade, bringing home a regular wage. He could feel pride and satisfaction in the casks he made, marked with his own personal blockmark. Elizabeth enjoyed a comfortable home. She and her parents were 'respectable'. She grew up morally strong, with a sense of hard work and thrift. One of her Sisters later wrote of her, 'refined, intelligent and gently nurtured, she knew nothing but the love of devoted parents, a comfortable and happy home and bright prospects for the future'. When she reached her twenty-first birthday on 2 September 1841, the world was at her feet.

Chapter Two

The Great Encounter

Six months later, however, an event occurred that was to turn her world upside down. On 18 February 1842 Blessed Dominic Barberi CP opened the first Passionist monastery in England at Aston Hall, scarcely two miles from the Prouts' doorstep. On 22 July that year he was joined by a young Passionist priest, Father Gaudentius Rossi.

Blessed Dominic's first three-week visit to England from 27 November 1840 and his final arrival on 5 October 1841 followed a quarter of a century of preparation and waiting, since he had been divinely assured in a mystical experience that he would be a Passionist priest and missioner in north-west Europe, particularly in England and its neighbouring kingdoms. In receiving those assurances, Blessed Dominic had become the heir to the mystical understanding given to St Paul of the Cross (1694–1775) that his Passionist 'children' would evangelize England.

Arrived in Aston Hall, Blessed Dominic soon arranged to say Mass and to give lectures in the Crown Inn on the High Street in Stone. He visited the Catholics in their homes. He organized Blessed Sacrament processions in the grounds of Aston Hall. He built a church school only about three minutes' walk from Elizabeth Prout's home. There was every possibility, as tradition has it, that she received the gift of the Catholic faith at a Benediction service in Aston or Stone. It was certainly in the context of Blessed Dominic's Stone and the missionary labours for which he became renowned that she became a Catholic at some time between 1842 and 1848. No definitive proof has so far been found to confirm the oral tradition in her Congregation that she was received into the Catholic Church by Blessed Dominic himself but circumstantial evidence corroborates this tradition. Certainly the Catholicism she received in both Aston and Stone was the spirituality of St Paul of the Cross as preached and practised by Blessed Dominic and the other Passionists there.

St Paul of the Cross had founded the Passionist Congregation in 1720 to live out and to preach the 'Memory' of the Passion of Jesus Christ. Seeing the Passion as the indisputable proof of Our Lord's infinitely overwhelming love for mankind, St Paul of the Cross saw Christians as baptized into the Crucified Christ. He wanted them to live out their 'Memory' of the Passion by offering their lives, too, in union with Christ, in the Eucharist, the Memorial of the Sacrifice of Calvary. By 'remembering' Our Lord's Passion in this way, Christians could unite their own sufferings with His and thus also share in His Resurrection. From her conversion to Catholicism in the Passionist parish of Stone, Elizabeth Prout's own life became an identification with Our Lord in His Passion. In her great encounter with Blessed Dominic Barberi, the Founder of the Passionists in England and the direct heir to the promises made to St Paul of the Cross, Elizabeth Prout, the future Foundress of the Sisters of the Cross and Passion, entered into her own Passionist inheritance.

After her conversion to Catholicism, Elizabeth came to know Father Ignatius Spencer CP, previously Father George Spencer, Spiritual Director in Oscott College and also the youngest son of the second Earl Spencer and thus uncle, several generations removed, to Princes William and Harry.

At the same time, she also came to know Father Gaudentius Rossi. In the spring of 1848 Father Gaudentius gave a mission in Northampton. During it he met the Sisters of the Infant Jesus, a Belgian teaching order that had arrived in England in 1845. When Father Gaudentius returned to Stone he told Elizabeth about these Sisters. In July 1848 she entered their novitiate. She was very happy in Northampton

5. Saint Paul of the Cross

6. Blessed Dominic Barberi CP

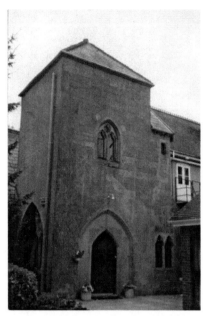

7. St Michael's Passionist Retreat, Aston Hall

8. Fr Gaudentius Rossi CP

9a. Blessed Dominic's Church School, Stone – exterior

9b. Blessed Dominic's Church School, Stone – interior

but by January 1849 she had developed tuberculosis in her knee. The doctor said she would never walk again and so she had to leave the convent. The time she had spent there, however, was very important for the work God intended her to do in the future. The Sisters had been very carefully instructed in catechetics by a Jesuit priest, Father Leblanc, and Elizabeth would have been trained in the same way. They had day schools for both the working and middle classes, as well as night classes for the girls who worked in the boot and shoe industry or other occupations during the day. As well as receiving religious instruction and a rudimentary education in literacy and numeracy, the girls were also taught needlework in sewing workrooms, so that they would not need to go into the factories, where both their virtue and their Catholic faith would be at risk. During her stay in Northampton, Elizabeth also learned how to recite the Little Office of the Blessed Virgin Mary and became acquainted with the structures and practices of religious life. Thus God prepared her for her own work as the foundress of a new Congregation. Equally significantly, she discovered that the Passionist spirituality that she had imbibed in Stone from Blessed Dominic was further enriched by her experience of living a Rule that, although specifically directed towards the Infancy of Christ, was also oriented towards His Passion. Like St Paul of the Cross and his Congregation, she thus learnt to link the Nativity, Infancy and Calvary.

She returned home to Stone, where her mother nursed her so well that she did walk again. When she began to go to Mass, however, fasting from midnight as was the practice at that time, her mother refused her any breakfast. Next she turned to shouting at her and finally struck her. Elizabeth realized that, if she wanted to be a Catholic, she would have to leave home.

Blessed Dominic died on 27 August 1849. Elizabeth probably attended his Requiem Mass in the church school he had built in Stone and then walked in the funeral procession to Aston Hall, where, after a burial service, he was interred under the sanctuary of the new St Michael's church. She applied for admission to a novitiate in Belgium and in the meantime, with the help of Father Gaudentius Rossi, she took up a teaching post in Manchester, regardless of the cholera that stalked its streets.

Chapter Three

Foundress of a New Type of Religious Order

Father Gaudentius was able to obtain this post for her because he had given a mission in St Chad's, Cheetham Hill in Manchester in early 1849. During it the parish priest, Father Robert Croskell, had told him that he was looking for a schoolmistress. They had also discussed the need for a religious order for women of the lower middle and working classes, who could not afford the dowries required by the established orders. When Blessed Dominic had died, Father Ignatius Spencer had succeeded him as Provincial Superior. Father Ignatius gave Father Gaudentius permission to co-operate with Father Croskell in founding the type of order they had discussed.

Elizabeth arrived in Manchester, the frontier town of the industrial revolution, about early September 1849. In addition to teaching in St Chad's girls' school, she started a kind of girls' sodality, where she taught the young Catholic mill girls their religion, as well as how to sew and knit, read, write and count, and to have fun and games too. She gave her spare time to looking after the sacristy in St Chad's church. Fathers Croskell and Gaudentius invited her to be the Foundress of their projected new order. Their invitation coincided with a letter of acceptance from the Belgian novitiate and she had also received a marriage proposal. She would not hear of marriage but she could have gone to Belgium. Instead she made a radical option for the poor. She agreed to co-operate in the foundation of the new order. Thus she selflessly abandoned her opportunity to retry her religious vocation in the security of an established convent.

Her decision was particularly courageous because she had already had some experience of the social conditions of Manchester. Although she lodged at 58 Stocks Street, beside St Chad's church in the respectable area of Cheetham Hill, Elizabeth had to go down into the centre of Manchester to teach. St Chad's church was a new one built in a developing area to replace the previous church in Rook Street in central Manchester, where the old buildings were being demolished. St Chad's schools, however, were still in the centre of the town, so that Elizabeth taught in George Leigh Street in the factory area of Ancoats. Here the workers lived in rows and rows of brick houses, built back to back and often forming courtyards which were entered through dark, narrow alleys.

On her way to George Leigh Street, Elizabeth would also have seen Angel Meadow, which formed part of St Chad's new parish but, as Manchester's worst slum, presented a sharp contrast to the new housing around Stocks Street. The houses in Angel Meadow were larger than those in Ancoats, because they had been built for the middle classes. As their occupants had moved out to the healthier suburbs, however, these large houses had been turned into rented-room accommodation and common mixed lodging houses. A journalist in 1849 described Angel Meadow as 'the lowest, most filthy, most unhealthy and most wicked locality in Manchester', 'full of cellars', 'the home of prostitutes, their bullies, thieves, cadgers, vagrants, tramps and, in the very worst sties of filth and darkness, the unhappy wretches', Irish famine refugees from Westport in County Mayo. Crowded into cellars and lying on rags, shavings or straw, they lived on potatoes, meal and scraps begged on the streets. Father Sheehan of St Chad's described the area in 1850 as 'the most densely populated part of the town, where the poorest, the less educated and the most criminal members of the community' resided. One and a half miles in length and a mile wide, it had a population of 15,000 Catholics, 'chiefly employed as handloom weavers, hawkers and factory opera-tives, the poorest members of the community'. Conditions were especially bad because the people had to share common privies, ashpits and water pumps located in the courts or along the streets. Very often the owners of the properties neglected to repair either houses or amenities, with the result that homes were damp, conveniences became unusable and people had no water. Because of this basic deprivation, fever and other diseases were constant hazards; filth and smells commonplace. There were other nuisances, too. Round the corner from the Catholic infants' school in Dyche Street, someone kept a donkey beside his dwelling. Its 'affluvia', it was commented, caused 'the most noxious smell even in the next house'. St Michael's old graveyard was also in the vicinity. On 17 October 1849 the *Manchester Guardian* pointed out it had been full, and therefore closed, since 1842. Its condition was 'indecent', the newspaper claimed, and fraught with 'serious and prejudicial consequences to the health of the neighbourhood, a very poor and populous part of the town'. The corpses were scarcely covered, the coffins almost protruding from the soil.

As Elizabeth Prout and the Catholics of Angel Meadow made their way to St Chad's church, they had to pass along Ashley Lane beside the 'dirty and crowded pile of dilapidated old buildings called Gibraltar', described by the Manchester and Salford Sanitary Association as 'peculiarly notorious as a fertile source of fever'. Here twenty pigs were kept in a small open space. Ashley Lane itself was a steep hill. Apart from boding ill for Elizabeth Prout's tubercular knee, it was so dangerous that every day and at times every hour horses fell and were lamed as they struggled up it. Then there was the River Irk, one of Manchester's natural sewers, and a weir that created a pool of stagnant water. Although the stench of both in summertime warned of the danger of disease, entrepreneurs remained indifferent to these hazards to public health.

Elizabeth would quickly have realized that in fact Manchester's whole environment was unhealthy. Apart from the pollution from tanneries and dyeworks, there were about five hundred mill chimneys belching out black smoke, while the heavy rainfall and the mist from the low-lying rivers created so damp an atmosphere that bronchial and pulmonary complaints were inevitable. Elizabeth's first encounter with Manchester could only have convinced her that it might be, as Benjamin Disraeli claimed, the 'most wonderful city of modern times' but it was certainly, as the historian Professor Briggs would later describe it, the 'shock city of the age'. Elizabeth also founded her order against a background of Evangelical anti-Catholicism. These Evangelicals had a number of outstanding preachers, one of whom, Canon Hugh Stowell, lived in Salford. Through his lectures and a newspaper, the *Protestant Witness*, Stowell played a conspicuous role in fomenting both anti-Catholicism and anti-Irish activities in the area. His followers were particularly active in nearby Ashton-under-Lyne and Stockport. Moreover, Elizabeth's foundation also coincided with the anti-Catholic disturbances which followed the restoration of the Catholic hierarchy in England and Wales in 1850 and with attempts to pass parliamentary legislation for the inspection of convents.

Against this background, Elizabeth Prout courageously opened her first convent at 69 Stocks Street on 15 August 1851, the feast of Our Lady's Assumption, a feast very dear to St Paul of the Cross. Her option for the poor was real, because her first two companions comprised a powerloom weaver and a domestic servant, who left that occupation to join the other in the mill, and both were Irish immigrants. As described by a later annalist, 'They rose at 4.00 in the morning and after having performed the prescribed devotions, namely one half hour of meditation and some vocal prayers, they performed whatever domestic duties required to be done.' Since the two other Sisters left at 5.30 a.m. to be in the mill by 6.00, Elizabeth finished tidying the house and left for school at 8.30. Each took some food for lunch and they had a meal together in the evening. Father Croskell visited them in the evenings, too, to instruct them in the duties of religious life. He also presided over the private ceremony they had in the Lady Chapel of St Chad's church on 2 February 1852, known at that time as the feast of Our Lady's Purification and now as Our Lord's Presentation or

Candlemas. From then they wore a black dress as a sign of their religious dedication. As more postulants arrived in 1852, sectarian rivalry erupted in the infamous Stockport Riots, in which two Catholic churches were devastated, the tabernacles smashed open and the Sacred Hosts scattered, the priest's house and twenty-four Catholic homes gutted and a hundred people seriously wounded, one even dead. Catholics in Manchester feared for their lives and properties.

Although one or two of Elizabeth's new companions were able to teach, the others were seamstresses. Since all the first Sisters' occupations were notoriously overworked and underpaid, she founded her Congregation in deep poverty. It was rich in spirituality, however. Father Croskell shared in the foundation but, as he later insisted, he left the formation of its spirit and its special direction to the Passionist, Father Gaudentius Rossi. In writing the Rule in 1852, Father Gaudentius inculcated the same virtues and the same 'Memory' that St Paul of the Cross had given to the Passionist Congregation. Since he had no authority from the Passionist Father General to give them the title, 'Sisters of the Cross and Passion', he called them 'Sisters of the Holy Family', a title that was resonantly Passionist in reflecting a devotion practised by St Paul of the Cross and part of the heritage of his Congregation. Father Gaudentius also legislated for a rich devotional life in keeping with Passionist practices and with the Tridentine reforms that Cardinal Wiseman was then promoting in England. He also constantly stressed the need for 'continual, sincere and fervent prayer'.

> I beg again and again to repeat, [he told Elizabeth in October 1852] that the spirit of the Institute is a spirit of recollection and mental prayer joined with manual labour and other external occupations and that mental prayer or meditation ought to be attended to with all possible care and attention.

Since this religious contemplative life formed the heart, the *raison d'être* of the new Congregation, Father Gaudentius did not legislate for any specific apostolate. Provided that the Sisters could earn their living, so that the Congregation would be self-supporting, they could do any kind of work consonant with its spirit and their talents. He did envisage, however, that, as far as possible, they would not go out to work. Although they had to continue to work in the mills and sewing houses at the beginning, he wanted them to have an industrial workroom in the convent. Similarly, although the needs of the Church in the Manchester area necessitated their going out to teach in parish schools, Father Gaudentius envisaged that in the future the Sisters would have their own schools in or adjacent to the convent. They were also to instruct converts, directed to them by the parish priest, and they could allow women to come to the convent for retreats. In a significant reflection of the parish visitation that the Passionist Fathers and Brothers conducted during their parish missions, he legislated for an active apostolate outside the convent in parish visitation of the poor and spiritually needy in their homes, in order to inculcate the 'Memory' of the Holy Family and the Passion, to encourage the people to come to Mass and to persuade parents to send their children to a Catholic school.

Chapter Four

An Apostolate in Education

From her first arrival in Manchester in late 1849, Elizabeth Prout played an important role in safeguarding Catholic schools against the current attacks of secularists and political economists. Manchester was the world's first industrial city. Its capitalists, proud of their economic and commercial achievements, strove to enhance their cultural amenities too. They also wanted to improve their educational facilities, even to having their own university, and they wanted to provide a system of rudimentary education that would ensure that their manual workers understood their role in industrial society. England was not a democracy in 1849. It was a class society. By 1849 these prestigious Manchester men were pressing for rate-supported education, so that even the poorest children could learn to read, write and count. They did not intend to provide religious education. They claimed that it led immediately to denominational wrangling and in any case it could be given at Sunday schools. Their proposals were hotly debated in Manchester, even after they had been rejected by parliament. Then, in January 1851, the Evangelical Canon Stowell and other members of the Manchester and Salford Committee on Education produced their own suggestions for rate-supported schools. They proposed that religion should be taught from the seventeenth-century King James Authorized Version of the Bible. No school that refused to use that Version could be eligible for rate support. Thus they excluded the Catholics and the Jews. They also proposed to build some new Protestant schools, which would be rate-supported and therefore free, in such largely Catholic areas as Angel Meadow, Ancoats and Deansgate. As a result, working-class Catholics would have a choice of free attendance at the Protestant schools, where they would probably lose their Catholic faith; fee-paying attendance at Catholic schools; or continued illiteracy because of their acute poverty. In the face of this threat, the Catholic clergy were desperate to find teachers to open Catholic schools in the working-class districts and to keep them open as cheaply as possible. This was why Father Croskell in 1849 was looking for a schoolmistress and why he was so pleased to welcome Elizabeth Prout to St Chad's. There was also another reason. From 1847 the Committee of Council on Education was willing to make government grants to Catholic schools, provided that they were open for inspection and reached governmental minimum standards. In 1849 St Chad's clergy wanted Elizabeth Prout to take charge of their girls' school so that it could be inspected. They could then apply for a government grant for books and equipment. They could also apply for a building grant for a new school to be built beside the new church at Stocks Street.

Elizabeth's classroom was in an old, long, low-ceilinged warehouse in only tolerable condition. Using the monitorial system of the time, she taught a daily average of at least a hundred girls. They were of mixed ability, with an age range of between eight and thirteen. Some were full-timers, others sleepy but obstreperous half-timers who worked in the cotton mills for half the day. Many of them came in ragged clothing, their eyes heavy from lack of sleep, their faces old beyond their years, their dishevelled hair covered with cotton fluff. Some came as it suited them. Some disappeared for weeks at a time, because, as the inspector commented, they could not resist the temptation to earn 6d a week selling chips, periwinkles or matches, in order to add a few loaves to the attenuated store of the starving family at home. Elizabeth's resources were meagre. The government inspection took place on 5 March 1850. Although the inspector praised Elizabeth's discipline and thought her organization was fair, he had to comment that the furniture was only moderate and her books and apparatus rather scanty. Her willingness to co-operate in this inspection, in spite of the poor conditions in which she was placed, was typical of the selfless availability she constantly demonstrated in the interests of the Church and of the poor. In spite of the deficiencies he noted, the inspector's report was so favourable that St Chad's received a grant for books and equipment and a building grant of £620. Thus Elizabeth Prout not only safeguarded the interests of the Catholic children in Ancoats by keeping open the George Leigh Street school: she also made an outstanding contribution towards a new school for the poor of Angel Meadow.

When the new school was completed in November 1851, however, St Chad's clergy, anxious to secure the permanent services of a well-established teaching order, invited the Sisters of Notre Dame to take charge of it. Elizabeth seems to have been asked to open the infant school in Dyche Street, in the heart of Angel Meadow, where small children were left, as one educationalist complained, to run wild and implike, in dirt and rags, round St Michael's graveyard, to roam the streets and, inevitably, to be lost or to be drawn into criminal activities. In taking charge of the infant school, Elizabeth once again made a deliberate option for the poor. All she saw of the new St Chad's, for which she had worked so hard, was in the night school as a supply teacher in the summer of 1852. In taking those classes for the mill girls, however, Elizabeth was once again keeping the Catholic night school open and thus safeguarding the interests and the Catholic faith of the working classes of Manchester.

About September 1852 one of Elizabeth's postulants took charge of the infant school in Dyche Steet. Elizabeth and another Sister then obliged Father Formby of St Mary's by going to teach in his parish school. It consisted of a few miserable rented rooms in a cottage in Royton Street, one of the ill-favoured streets off Deansgate. According to the curate, Father Henry Browne, in 1853 St Mary's had about 7,000 parishioners over a radius of three miles at the very centre of the city. Most were the labouring poor, chiefly employed in mills, living in back streets and cellars and, even more unfortunately, in a locality noted for wickedness and crime. St Mary's church, like St Chad's, was a new one, opened in 1848 on the site of an earlier church built in 1794. Blessed Dominic Barberi had preached in the old St Mary's in 1843. Father Ignatius Spencer attended the opening of the new church in 1848. Father Gaudentius Rossi gave four missions in the parish between 1849 and 1852. Royton Street lay in a highly industrialized area, where the people's dwellings were mixed indiscriminately with slaughterhouses, textile mills and timber yards. What would have struck Elizabeth Prout, however, was that there was a gin palace at every corner and the largest palaces were in the poorest streets. She would also have noticed the number of children sitting on steps, rolling on the cobbled roadway and dashing round the streets, their hair, as described by a Mancunian of the time, long, rough and uncombed, their clothes in rags, their hands and faces filthy and their feet, in most cases, presenting a dry coating of dirt, as though they had not been washed from birth. Here, in what the clergy described as the ruined and ill-ventilated rooms in Royton Street, Elizabeth Prout engaged in what an educationalist of the time described as the almost hopeless struggle with the poverty-stricken ignorance and semi-barbarism of Deansgate. It was well known, however, that the Catholic children of St Mary's, when attired in the white dresses and lace caps supplied by the parish for the Whit Walks, could process in such splendour, with banners and bands, that the whole of Manchester turned out to admire them. By teaching in St Mary's day and Sunday schools, Elizabeth Prout safeguarded the Catholic position in that working-class district. It was at great cost to herself, however, for twice each day, and even four times on Sundays, she had to limp the considerable distance between Deansgate and Cheetham Hill. Poor to the point of near-destitution, in January 1853 she became seriously ill. When she recovered about April 1853, she opened a new school in St Joseph's parish, recently formed from a section of St Patrick's predominantly Irish area.

The parish priest of St Joseph's, Goulden Street, was

Father Stephan, one of the French priests who had come to help in Manchester during the Irish fever epidemic. He asked Elizabeth to open a school in his church building, which had previously been a temperance guild hall. Father Gaudentius agreed, on condition that Father Stephan provided desks, a stove to warm the room in winter, books, maps, ink and slates and so on. Having opened the school, Father Stephan wanted to apply for a government grant. Elizabeth therefore had to have another inspection of her teaching. When the inspector arrived to find a mixed class of 179 girls and boys, he regretted that the school was too poor to merit a grant. 'This very interesting school', he reported, 'situated in one of the poorest and most populous parts of Manchester, and crowded with children, is imperfectly furnished and ill supplied with indispensable requisites.' He was favourably impressed by Elizabeth Prout and her companion, however, for he continued, 'Nevertheless the children seem to attend with willingness and to be much attached to their two amiable teachers, who cannot fail to exercise a moral influence of high value.' Elizabeth would have transferred her convent from Stocks Street to St Joseph's parish but was unable to find a house that was not full of bugs.

In later 1853, however, all the Sisters except Elizabeth Prout caught fever and several almost died. It was clear that the house in Stocks Street was too small for their increasing numbers. Because of her deep poverty, most of the priests in Manchester thought that Elizabeth was foolish to try to found a religious order for the poor and so they gave her little sympathy when her Sisters were ill. A young Irish doctor, however, Dr J. Walsh, refused to take any fees. Father W. J. Daly of Newton Heath lent her his house while they recuperated. Then in April 1854 Bishop William Turner, the first Bishop of Salford, gave them a new convent in Levenshulme, then a developing suburb in the countryside outside Manchester. Elizabeth and her companion continued to teach in St Joseph's, walking the three miles each way every day until the winter approached, and then, because they could not afford to take transport, they had to leave the heart of Manchester.

In accordance with Father Gaudentius Rossi's Rule, as soon as possible after the first group of Sisters had received the religious habit in 1852, Elizabeth had withdrawn them from sewing houses and had established a workroom in the convent itself. At the beginning this made them poorer than ever, because they became slopworkers, the lowest-paid type of seamstresses. From about early 1854, however, they began to make church vestments for Thomas Brown and Company of Manchester. Thus they fulfilled a real apostolate in the Catholic revival of the time, when new churches were constantly being opened in the industrial areas. Once the community moved to Levenshulme, it became impossible for any of them to continue to work in the mills, which opened in the centre of Manchester at 6 a.m.

In Levenshulme, however, Elizabeth continued her apostolate in education. The convent was adjacent to St Mary's church, then situated in what became known in 1857 as Alma Park. In one of the adjacent farm buildings, converted into a school, she opened St Mary's elementary school for the children of the area, and within the convent she also opened a day and boarding school for girls. Thus she addressed another problem that lay behind the discrimination against Catholics inherent in the Manchester and Salford Committee's plans: the education of the upper working and middle classes, such as the shopkeepers, tradesmen and artisans. Elizabeth's school was particularly needed because the education of girls was coming to be seen as even socially necessary. As Cardinal Wiseman had expressed it, the English Catholic Church must rely on the women of the middle classes for its mothers, its religious, its benefactors of the poor, its nurses for the sick and dying and for its most useful helpers in every kind of good work. In establishing a fee-paying school at Levenshulme, Elizabeth was also providing a fixed income for her community and providing work within the convent for all her Sisters. Thus she could now concentrate on establishing the contemplative–active religious order envisaged by Father Gaudentius Rossi CP.

Chapter Five

The Sign of the Cross

Elizabeth Prout and her first six companions had received a black religious habit from Father Gaudentius Rossi CP, assisted by Father Croskell, in the convent in Stocks Street on 21 November 1852, the feast of the Presentation of Our Lady, which had always been regarded from the time of St Paul of the Cross as the birthday of the Passionist Congregation. Throughout the next two years she trained her novices in the knowledge and practice of the vows they would take and in the love of poverty, prayer and solitude that constituted the charism of the Passionist Congregation and lay at the heart of the Rule that Father Gaudentius had written for them in 1852. He was increasingly aware of Elizabeth's worth as Foundress.

> In regard to yourself personally, [he told her], I feel more and more convinced that God has chosen you as a guide to your Sisters and a housekeeper in the Holy Family. Almighty God has given you lights and grace and strength to go through many difficulties.

On 13 November 1854 Elizabeth and five companions began a retreat under his direction in preparation for taking their vows. Preaching to them three times each day, Father Gaudentius noted the deep attention and even emotion with which they listened. At last the day arrived that Elizabeth had longed for since she had first felt called to religious life, the day on which she could give herself totally to her Crucified

10. Bishop William Turner, first Bishop of Salford

Spouse. It had seemed for a time that such was not, after all, God's will for her. This day had come now only after many uncertainties, vicissitudes and incredible hardships. It had come, however, and on 21 November 1854, as Bishop Turner held up the Sacred Host during Mass, Elizabeth Prout made her first profession of vows in St Mary's church, Levenshulme. From then she was known as Mother Mary Joseph of Jesus. She wore a black habit and veil, on her right hand a silver ring bearing a Cross and the initials 'JMJ' for 'Jesus, Mary and Joseph' and over her heart the Passionist Sign, except that the words 'JESU XPI PASSIO' were replaced by the letters 'JMJ'.

In this adaptation Elizabeth Prout took as much as she dared of the Passionist Sign of St Paul of the Cross. Father Gaudentius had not been able to give her Congregation either the Passionist title or the Passionist Rule in its entirety, because only the Passionist Father General could confer such privileges, as he later did. Father Gaudentius, nevertheless,

11. The Passionist Sign

had given a title with a Passionist connotation and a Rule that
was fundamentally Paulacrucian. Similarly, in discussing with
her the distinctive Badge the Sisters would wear after profession, Father Gaudentius had suggested a Cross above the
letters 'JMJ'. His suggestion carried a specific Passionist
significance. The particular charism of St Paul of the Cross
as the Founder of the Passionist Congregation sprang from a
mystical experience in 1720. As he described it, he was
'raised up in God in the deepest recollection, with complete
forgetfulness of all else and with great interior peace'. At
that moment, he saw himself clothed in a long, black garment
with a white Cross on his breast. Below the Cross the Holy
Name of Jesus was written in white letters. At that instant
he heard a voice say, 'This signifies how pure and spotless
that heart should be which must bear the Holy Name of Jesus
engraven upon it.' Paul left his home to found his
Congregation on 21 November 1720 and was clothed by
Bishop Gattinara of Alessandria in the long, black tunic. He
was not allowed to wear the Sign, however, until 1741, when

he received papal approbation of his Rule. By that time he had a clearer understanding that his Congregation's unique charism, its distinctive vocation in the Church, was to live the 'Memory' of the Passion and to preach Christ Crucified. The Sign that he then gave his followers bore the white Cross with the inscription, within a white heart, 'JESU XPI PASSIO', the 'Passion of Jesus Christ' in Hebrew, Greek and Latin, above three nails. When, in 1854, Father Gaudentius made his own suggestion to Elizabeth Prout, he was recalling the Sign of Paul's 1720 mystical experience. Elizabeth went further. In devising her adaptation, which she embroidered herself, and especially in taking the three nails, which Father Gaudentius had not mentioned, she deliberately gave her Congregation a Sign that was as Passionist as she could make it.

Once the first group of Sisters had completed their novitiate, Elizabeth was able to expand her Congregation. At the request of Father John Quealy, the parish priest of St Ann's, Ashton-under-Lyne, she made her first new opening there about New Year's Day, 1855. Ashton was notorious for its sectarian rivalry, provoked by Orangeism, Irish Ribbonism and the Evangelicals. It had a population of 30,000, of whom about 4,000 were Catholics. According to Father Gaudentius, who had given a mission there in 1854, they were exclusively composed of working people, the majority employed in the cotton mills. Many of them were Irish refugees. Too poor to pay the rent for better housing, they either stayed in the common lodging houses or rented the worst houses in the town, infested by vermin. Elizabeth Prout, now Mother Mary Joseph, and Sister Mary Paul Taylor opened a school for three hundred children in St Ann's church school. They and two other Sisters visited the sick and sought out and instructed negligent Catholics. They had great influence amongst the people and their work prospered.

Even before going to Ashton, Elizabeth had considered a foundation in Sutton, near St Helens. Blessed Dominic Barberi and Father Ignatius Spencer had chosen a site there in 1849, at the invitation of the local railway magnate, John

Smith, and he had then erected St Anne's church, monastery and school. In 1854 the Rector of St Anne's, Father Bernardine Carosi CP, invited Elizabeth to take charge of St Anne's girls' school. The invitation signified far more than a further step in her educational apostolate. It represented a recognition on the part of the Passionist Congregation in England that her Congregation had a special affinity with the sons of St Paul of the Cross. The difficulty about Sutton, however, was that it was in the Liverpool rather than the Salford Diocese. Bishop Turner had no jurisdiction there and he was anxious to have the Sisters in his own parishes. Elizabeth therefore had gone to Ashton. In 1855, however, the Misses Orrell of Blackbrook were looking for a new headmistress for Parr Hall, a ladies' academy under their patronage. At Father Bernardine's suggestion, Elizabeth Prout was invited to open a convent in Parr Hall, to take charge of the academy and to open day and Sunday schools for the working-class children at Blackbrook. Elizabeth accepted the invitation with the approval of Bishop Turner, of the Bishop of Liverpool, of Father Gaudentius Rossi and of Father Ignatius Spencer. She reduced the fees at Parr Hall in order to open the school to those Catholic middle and upper working-class girls who were so badly in need of educational provision. She admitted day pupils and she introduced a school uniform to eradicate class distinctions in dress. She also opened St Helen's parish school and a Sunday school for the children of Blackbrook, as well as taking charge of St Anne's girls' school in Sutton. In September 1855 she opened another convent in Sutton itself. In 1857 her Sisters took charge of the new St Joseph's school at Peasley Cross. In making these foundations, Elizabeth extended her apostolate in education; she took her religious Congregation into a second diocese; and she started a tradition of direct partnership with the Passionist Congregation, which has remained unbroken ever since.

It was inevitable that such enterprise should evoke additional difficulties and the cross was never absent from the life of Elizabeth Prout. She was often ill, even seriously, and

12. Holy Cross Convent, Peckers Hill Road, Sutton

there was always the harsh, daily grind in both her penitential contemplative lifestyle and her demanding active apostolate. In addition, two or three Sisters, who regarded Father Gaudentius rather than herself as their superior, constantly flouted her authority, creating discord in the community. Her position was especially difficult because the ringleader, Sister Clare, had come to the order with the reputation of being a living saint and Father Gaudentius esteemed her highly. When Elizabeth opened her new foundation at Ashton, Sister Clare, who was already the novice mistress, had also become the superior of Levenshulme. In November 1855 Father Gaudentius was sent to North America. Sister Clare then became unsettled and wanted to leave. According to a contemporary annalist, writing later, she caused trouble in a variety of ways. By 1857 she had plunged the Congregation into serious debt. Then she left, followed by several others. Elizabeth repeated the words of St Paul of the Cross and Blessed Dominic Barberi, 'Few and good. Few and good.'

> She would not allow the slightest deviation in the Rule, [wrote
> an annalist] or in regular observance. She showed by her own
> example and also by those who persevered with her that to
> those who really loved God there was nothing impossible in
> the Rule and Customs. She would not allow on any account
> the active work of the Sisters to interfere with their spiritual
> observances.

The 'active work of Martha' must in no way interfere with or
set aside the 'contemplation of Mary'. Short of Sisters,
however, she had to close her flourishing foundations at Parr
Hall and Ashton. When the Catholics of Ashton heard that the
Sisters were leaving, there was widespread grief and conster-
nation. They could be pacified only by Elizabeth's promising
to send them back when their numbers increased and the
opportunity presented itself.

In the meantime, with Bishop Turner's approval and a gener-
ous donation, Elizabeth Prout had to go out to beg round the
Salford Diocese. The 1857 worldwide financial crisis, however,
was then being felt in redundancies and short time in
Lancashire's cotton industry, so that, although she travelled all
over Lancashire, she found that the people had little to give.

Father Ignatius Spencer wrote to Irish bishops for permission for her to quest in Ireland. Taking with her an Irish
Sister, Sister Catherine Scanlon, she crossed from Liverpool
to Dublin on 24–25 November 1855. Father Ignatius Spencer
was already there. He found them lodgings with a Miss Nolan
at 43 Dorset Street and they quested in Dublin for the next
two or three weeks. There were, however, already numerous
collections for new churches, schools, orphanages and hospi-
tals. For Elizabeth, as she met with many repulses, hard
words and suchlike humiliations, to quote an annalist, there
seemed little chance of help. As the weather changed first to
dull and then to a great gale, she must have felt it accorded
with her despair. The rain came down in torrents. The wind
roared. Slates and chimney pots were scattered over Dublin's
streets. Then there was a hurricane, threatening the ships on
the River Liffey. An eighty-foot chimney crashed down on
the quays. Railways were badly damaged and the

Liverpool–Dublin crossing was cancelled because of mountainous waves. There was no turn of the tide for Elizabeth. There were so many collections in Dublin that her own appeal was virtually a non-starter. On 13 December Father Ignatius Spencer had a good chat with her and the next day she and Sister Catherine set out for Borrisokane, near the family home at Aglish of Margaret Reddan, who had entered her novitiate shortly after Father Ignatius and other Passionists had given a mission there in 1855. From Borrisokane they went southwards to Cork, Sister Catherine's home ground. They stayed at the South Presentation Convent while questing in Cork City. Then they went to the Presentation Convent in Fermoy and from there quested in the neighbouring towns and countryside. They received the greatest kindness from priests and people and always a most hearty welcome from the Presentation Nuns. After a number of weeks they returned to Dublin, where they visited the Passionists in Mount Argus before crossing back to England on 27 January 1858, only to discover that the Sister whom Elizabeth had left in charge had neglected the community and was preparing to enter an enclosed order.

Not content with the damage they had already caused, the ex-Sisters spread such calumnies that in 1858 Canon Croskell withdrew from the affairs of the Congregation. Elizabeth personally was placed in a very dangerous position because of contemporary opposition to religious institutes. One of the features of the Gothic revival was the publication of a number of 'medieval' romances, depicting monks and nuns as ogres and kidnappers. Transferred from the pages of fiction into the Evangelical newspapers, these weird tales caught the imagination of popular Protestantism. Confessors were depicted as immoral, superiors as tyrants and as murderers of rebellious nuns. Convents were depicted as beehives of secret dungeons and burial holes. Even worse, several Evangelicals tried to produce parliamentary legislation for the inspection of convents. All female religious houses were to be registered and were to be inspected twice a year, without warning, and any nun could be transferred at a moment's notice to the workhouse. Anyone who tried to obstruct the entrance of the inspectors would be liable to ten years' transportation or two years' hard labour in prison. Any nun who refused to co-operate would be liable to a fine or twelve months' hard labour. This legislation was never passed but several nuns, both Catholic and Anglican, had to face public accusations. Elizabeth Prout's position was very serious.

Fortunately, the Passionist Rector of Broadway in Worcestershire, Father Bernard O'Loughlin, arrived in Levenshulme to give the Sisters' annual retreat and to receive the vows of four novices as the opposition reached its climax. When he went to ask Provost Croskell for faculties during the retreat, the Provost told him that the Congregation was about to be suppressed, because it was not self-supporting. It seemed that the attempt to provide consecrated religious life for lower-class women was an economic failure. There were other charges too. Father Bernard said he could not give the retreat under such circumstances, much less receive the novices' vows. Bishop Turner, therefore, immediately appointed four canons to hold an investigation. Provost Croskell asked Father Bernard to attend the hearings, which took place on 6 July 1858 in Levenshulme convent. The canons reported their findings to Bishop Turner the next morning and Father Bernard went to see him at noon. They met outside the Bishop's house. Manifesting 'the greatest pleasure and satisfaction', Bishop Turner immediately exclaimed, 'Well, Father Bernard, I have good news for you. The canons are satisfied with the investigation. The Institute is to continue and now the canons will in future be in favour of them.' After giving him a detailed report, he sent Father Bernard back to the convent to tell the Sisters the good news, to sing the *Te Deum* in thanksgiving and to give Solemn Benediction. Elizabeth communicated her joyous relief to her friend, Father Salvian Nardocci, the Passionist novice-master in Broadway. 'Now we are as firm as any other modern order in the Church', thanks to 'good Father Bernard'. Nevertheless, although Elizabeth and her Sisters were exonerated on every charge, they remained in financially straitened circumstances. Their darkest hour, however, was the prelude to the dawn.

When Father Gaudentius Rossi had been sent to North America in 1855, he had left Father Ignatius Spencer as the Sisters' Director. 'I have great confidence in him,' Father Gaudentius told Elizabeth, 'and full confidence in his personal virtue or rather extraordinary sanctity.' Apart from having given Father Gaudentius the initial permission to found the Congregation, Father Ignatius Spencer had entered directly into its affairs on 1 January 1854, when he arrived at the Sisters' temporary convent at Newton Heath. During the next eight days, as the arctic conditions of a terrible snowstorm enveloped Manchester and much of England, Father Ignatius gave the Sisters a retreat that centred totally on Our Lord's Passion. He gave them another in the summer of 1855, after which he was largely instrumental in bringing them to Sutton and Parr Hall. From Father Gaudentius Rossi's departure for North America, Father Ignatius was indefatigable on their behalf. Told of the impending defections in 1857, he wrote to Elizabeth,

Do you not see that this is the time of trial? If they wish to kick, bite and run, let them. The children of Blessed Paul [of the Cross] did the same, so did the children of St Francis but God gave them others more faithful and worthy and so He will give you. If they all go, 'God speed them': we can begin again with God's blessing.

As one of the annalists recorded, 'His confidence in the order was so great that he sent postulants when to all human appearances it would be broken up in a few weeks' time, for all the powers of hell seemed to be combined against it.' As a result, with the troublemakers gone and some excellent candidates in the novitiate, the Congregation gained a new lease of life, mainly owing to the efforts of Father Ignatius Spencer. In 1857 he had taken Father Gaudentius Rossi's Rule to Rome for the approval of the Holy See. He was told that, whilst the obect of the Congregation was excellent, the Rule was too diffuse. He was told to condense it and to base it on the Rule of a sainted founder. That could, of course, be no other than St Paul of the Cross. In 1862–3 he and Elizabeth Prout applied themselves to that task, as he was returning to Rome in 1863. It would have been only then, when she read the Passionist Rule for the first time, that Elizabeth would have realized that in fact, in spite of Father Gaudentius Rossi's rearrangement and devotional embellishments, she had in fact already been following a basically Passionist Rule since 1852. The Holy See may also have asked for a definition of the active apostolate for which the Congregation was being founded. Father Gaudentius had emphasized the 'Memory' of the Holy Family, which highlighted its contemplative nature. Although some of the Sisters taught and others made vestments, Father Gaudentius had not defined any active apostolate as the specific reason for the Congregation's foundation. It therefore fell to Elizabeth Prout and Father Ignatius Spencer to decide on its primary active apostolate. They defined it as the provision of Homes, or refuges, for factory girls. Elizabeth, like Father Gaudentius earlier, had no authority to take the Passionist Rule, the Sign or the habit in their entirety. In 1853, however, she had asked to have St Paul of the Cross as the patron of her Congregation. She had always consistently sought the spiritual guidance of the Passionist Fathers in confessions, retreats, clothings and professions and most recently in transferring her novitiate to the Passionist environment of Sutton. Now, in 1862–3, assisted by Father Ignatius Spencer, she directed her Congregation in the Rule itself to a more specifically Passionist identity. The Sisters' Passionist charism was so obvious that when the Passionist Father General, Father Peter Paul Cayro, visited Sutton shortly after her death in 1864, he immediately invited them to be aggregated to the Passionist Congregation under the name 'Sisters of the Cross and Passion'. Restrictions in Rome, on account of the War of Italian Unification, prevented that from being accomplished until 1874, but the Sisters were actually known as the Sisters of the Cross and Passion from 1864. When Father Alphonsus O'Neill presented each Sister with the full Passionist Sign in April 1875, Elizabeth Prout's own desires came to fruition.

Chapter Six

A New Social Apostolate

Elizabeth Prout had been conscious of the needs of the mill girls since she had first arrived in Manchester in 1849. She knew of the general hazards to health from their conditions of work, the dangers from unfenced machinery and the immorality said to be prevalent amongst them. She knew, too, that, because of their long hours of work, girls employed in the factories could never learn to knit, sew, cook or wash. As wives and mothers they were so unacquainted with the duties of housewifery that they did not know how to care for their own children. In the mid years of the nineteenth century, their hours of work were reduced so that they would have time to improve their homes, attend night classes and enjoy some recreation. Unfortunately there were few forms of innocent recreation available. A journalist of the time wrote that he had never witnessed more open, brutal and general intemperance than he saw in the Ancoats area of Manchester in 1849. The streets swarmed with drunken men and women, while young mill girls and boys romped and shouted with each other. The public houses and gin shops were full. There were rows, fights, scuffles inside and out and shouting, screaming and swearing mingled with the noise of half a dozen bands. Elizabeth Prout was very prompt in seeing and answering this situation. One of the annalists recorded that she and some friends gathered together young Catholic girls from the mills and workshops to give them instructions in their Catholic faith, lessons in needlework and means of innocent recreation, thus keeping them away from the dancing houses, low places of amusement and other dangerous occasions of sin. It was the Lancashire Cotton Famine, however, that caused Elizabeth to commit her Congregation to the care of the factory girls and that enabled her to keep her promise to return to Ashton-under-Lyne.

Just as Elizabeth Prout and Father Ignatius Spencer were beginning their work on the revision of the Rule in 1862, the effects of the American Civil War were being felt in the Cotton Famine that gripped the Lancashire cotton towns, and none more than Ashton-under-Lyne. Sir James Kay Shuttleworth, Vice-Chairman of the Central Executive Relief Committee, devised a scheme by which the unemployed workers could receive poor relief in return for attending educational classes. Sewing classes were started where the factory girls could learn reading, writing and arithmetic in the mornings and sewing and knitting in the afternoons. In late October 1862, Father Cromblehome, parish priest of St Ann's, was looking for Catholic teachers so that he could establish these classes for his unemployed parishioners. With Bishop Turner's approval, he asked Father Ignatius Spencer and Elizabeth Prout if she could send Sisters back to Ashton to provide these schools. Both she and her community were delighted at being able to help the mill girls and Elizabeth could agree without hesitation because they would be paid for their work. Accordingly she arranged for four Sisters to go to Ashton. However, when Father Ignatius arrived with the first two Sisters on 22 November, they discovered there was nothing ready for them except an empty house. When Elizabeth arrived with two other Sisters the next day and found that even then nothing had been done to provide for them, she almost took them back to Sutton. Father Ignatius Spencer's pleas prevented her but in November's keen winds she caught a bad cold, which was particularly serious because of her tubercular condition. During the next year, however, the Sisters' work was very much appreciated in Ashton-under-Lyne. Some of the mill girls had never held a needle before. Now they learnt how to make clothes, which they could keep at reduced prices or sell to others. They received food and, although their payment was not as high as their customary wages, they did receive some remuneration and they were employed. Their dignity as well as their livelihood was safeguarded. There was great competition to attend these sewing classes, so that, by coming to their aid, Elizabeth Prout performed a very real service for almost six hundred mill girls, a substantial proportion of the female operatives in the town's schools. The Mayor of Ashton visited them frequently. He expressed his approval very warmly, saying that the conduct and work of the girls in the Sisters' classes were highly superior to those in any other sewing school in the town. He expressed a wish that the Sisters would also take charge of a department in the hospital. Whilst endorsing his wish for the future, however, Elizabeth was more immediately concerned to open a Home for mill girls.

There was no doubt of the need for such Homes. Wages in the mills made girls of thirteen years of age so independent of their parents that they often left home to move into lodgings. Conditions inside the over-heated mills, where teenage boys and girls worked side by side, made them crave for drink and excite-ment with morally disastrous results. The need for a Home for Catholic mill girls was particularly pressing, because so many were Irish immigrants, forced to live in common mixed lodging houses, to the certain detriment of their virtue and open to petty persecution on account of both their religion and their race. In revising the Rule in 1862-3, therefore, Elizabeth and Father Ignatius wrote that, according to their means and opportunities, the Sisters would open houses of refuge, or Homes, for young women of the working classes in or near the large factory towns. The girls would be provided with food and lodging on moderate terms, on condition of complying with some degree of restraint and good discipline. The Sisters would treat them with motherly affection, provide for their comfort and cleanliness, instruct them in their Catholic faith and teach them both the duties of domestic life and the first elements of education. Elizabeth Prout was not an innovator in providing refuges for women at risk, for there were already several types in existence. She was different, however, in adding her own contemplative dimension. She did not offer simply a refuge, nor even just a home, valuable as they were. She offered the girls a modified kind of religious life. They could wear secular dress, continue to work in the mills and retain their wages, whilst living a community life with a prayerful dimension in the same house as the Sisters, although not within the enclosure and without binding themselves to a lifelong commitment to monastic observance or to the Sisters' other active apostolates. Father Cromblehome was delighted with the Sisters, considering them the best type of nuns for the purpose in hand. He was determined to build them a convent and a Home for factory girls. Since there was a tract of land close to the church and school, Father Ignatius Spencer went down to Leicestershire in the depths of winter and then to Dunham Massey to ask Lord Stamford, the landowner, to donate it for that purpose. Lord Stamford, however, supported the strong anti-Catholic element in Ashton-under-Lyne and so refused. Elizabeth, therefore, did not achieve her object in Ashton but she continued to hope that it would be possible to replace her Levenshulme convent with a Home for factory girls in one of Lancashire's industrial towns. In the event, she did not live to realize her ambition, for she died in January 1864, but later that year her Sisters opened a convent in Bolton for the express purpose of opening a Home for mill girls there and teaching in St Mary's school. The Home was opened in 1865, the first of several in the industrial north, as well as one in London and others in Ireland and abroad. The blessings of such Homes spread to society at large and to unknown thousands whose lives and future happiness were influenced by the mothers who had had the Sisters' training and care.

Chapter Seven

Identification with Christ in His Passion

In writing the Rule for Elizabeth Prout and her Sisters in 1852, Father Gaudentius Rossi had been fundamentally influenced by the Rule of St Paul of the Cross, the only Rule he knew, and consequently by the spirituality of St Paul of the Cross. The key to this spirituality is Paul's concept of the *Memoria Passionis* or the 'Memory' of the Passion. St Paul of the Cross used the word 'Memory' in the scriptural sense of re-living, re-experiencing, actually participating in, in one's own heart, as also understood in the scriptural sense of meaning in the depths of one's being. When he founded his Congregation to keep alive this 'Memory' of the Passion, he wanted its members to re-experience Our Lord's Passion, to be identified with Him in His Passion and to teach that same living 'Memory' to the people.

Elizabeth Prout's Congregation was founded against the background of all the excitement surrounding the process for the Beatification of Paul of the Cross, which took place in 1853. Both Father Gaudentius Rossi and Father Ignatius Spencer seem to have been familiar with the letters of St Paul of the Cross. Father Gaudentius would therefore have known that he often headed them 'JMJ' for 'Jesus, Mary and Joseph', just as Father Gaudentius himself did. Moreover, St Paul of the Cross had had a particular devotion to the Divine Nativity 'amid such lack of comfort and in such poverty'. The Nativity scene was one that he frequently referred to. 'I would like you to celebrate the holy feast of Christmas', he wrote in 1761, 'in the poor stable of your own heart, where the dear Jesus will be born in a spiritual way. Offer this poor stable to the holy Mary and to the holy St Joseph.' Devotion to the Holy Family was therefore an intrinsic part of Passionist spirituality right from the time of St Paul of the Cross. It was a devotion that Father Gaudentius would have had even as a Passionist. Hence it was not surprising that when he needed a title for Elizabeth and her Sisters he called them 'Sisters of the Holy Family'.

It was more than a title, however. In a letter of 21 December 1851, he told Elizabeth, 'All the Sisters should have a special devotion to these three great personages, Divine Jesus, Holy Mary and St Joseph.' In the Rule he wrote,

> The object of this new institution is to honour and to imitate in a special manner the mode of life of Our Divine Redeemer, His Blessed Virgin Mother and St Joseph in their house at Nazareth, where they were all diligently engaged in manual work and continual prayer.

Father Gaudentius, therefore, wanted the Sisters to live out the 'Memory' of the Holy Family in the same way as the Passionists lived out the 'Memory' of the Passion.

At the same time, in spite of making the Holy Family the central devotion of the Congregation, Father Gaudentius also inculcated devotion to the Sacred Passion. He seldom envisaged the Holy Family as consisting of Mary, Joseph and the Child Jesus. He invariably referred to Jesus as 'Our Divine Redeemer'. In his concept of the Holy Family Christ was an adult, or at least a teenager, since he spoke of his eighteen years in Nazareth; He was a worker; and, to the Sisters, He was their Divine Spouse. In times of sickness they were to imitate 'their Suffering Redeemer on the Cross'. They were to follow Him in their Obedience 'even to the death of the Cross' and they were 'to spend each Friday in pious remembrance and honour of the most bitter Passion of their Divine Spouse, Jesus Crucified', offering up 'all their good works, devout prayers and sufferings in union with the sufferings and prayers of their Divine Saviour' for the intention, unique to Passionists and a special inheritance from St Paul of the Cross, of the Conversion of England.

Elizabeth Prout's personal spirituality had been Passionist from her first encounter with Blessed Dominic Barberi. When she had to leave the novitiate in Northampton, Father Gaudentius had noted her peace and calm of mind and her perfect resignation to God's holy will. In February 1854, when, following the fever epidemic, one of her Sisters was again struck down with illness, he wrote, 'I most sincerely sympathise with you, my dear Sister Mary Joseph, for the large share of the Cross which Our Blessed Redeemer gives to you in different ways.' Elizabeth Prout wrote no spiritual treatises. She kept no diaries recording her spiritual favours. She claimed neither ecstasies nor visions. Father Gaudentius Rossi's letters offer occasional glimpses of spiritual consolations she had received but, for the most part, in her life as Foundress she epitomized in her own spiritual struggle the inherent conflict between the contemplative and the active that was so essential to her Congregation's Passionist spirituality. In February 1854 she told Father Gaudentius of her dryness in prayer and spiritual desolation. She was conscious of her sins and her wretchedness. She sincerely regretted what she considered her past negligent life, resolving with God's grace to correct herself. She made the resolution to do so every day but she felt she broke it every day, too. She longed to live for God alone but thought she never began. She lived by faith. Trying to help with a Levenshulme parish bazaar at the same time that she was checking Father Gaudentius Rossi's final version of his Rule and opening a new school for the working-class children of Blackbrook, she was utterly distracted. She felt a desire to pray continually but when she tried to reflect on Our Lord's Passion, within a minute or two she was overcome by distractions. She craved for solitude, longed to live in the presence of God, yearned to pray, was faithful to her times of prayer and yet she felt she never prayed. The Will of God, however, was always uppermost in her mind. The news that Father

Gaudentius was going to North America in 1855 struck her like a thunderclap and she felt his going keenly but, she told him, if God willed him to go, she must pray for generosity and courage. Like St Paul of the Cross, Elizabeth Prout received her strength from her reception of the sacraments and from the presence of the Blessed Sacrament, the Memorial of the Passion, in the convent chapel.

To the end of her life Elizabeth's sufferings were acute. From 1860 her mother was ill in Stone, as was Sister Zitta in Sutton. In February 1861 Sister Mary Cecilia dropped dead in Sutton of a heart attack. Sister Veronica died of tuberculosis in August 1861, Sister Zitta on 9 November. Anne Prout died, albeit as a Catholic, on 10 August 1862 and Edward Prout, happily restored to his Catholic faith, on 26 January 1863. Bowed down with humiliations, ill-health, defections, deaths and always the constant, harsh daily grind of hard work and deep poverty, Elizabeth Prout had learnt to love the Cross. Her own identification with Christ in His Passion was well expressed in a feastday card she gave to one of her Sisters in 1862:

> A cross no cross where Jesus is.
> With Jesus crosses are my bliss.
> Why should the cross so frighten me
> when on the Cross My God I see?

Father Ignatius Spencer took the revised Rule to Rome in April 1863. By then Elizabeth Prout's tuberculosis was reaching full development, as the serious cold that she had caught in Ashton-under-Lyne had kept its grip on her frail constitution. She had little chance to recover in Sutton, because the village lay in the throes of the poverty that emanated from the cotton famine. People who had previously been benefactors were now queuing up at the monastery door for food and no doubt there was another queue at the convent door. Few fees could have been paid in the schools, so that the Sisters had little income. With insufficient food and living in an environment heavily polluted by alkali works, Elizabeth

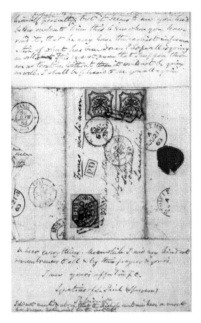

13. Letter from Fr Ignatius Spencer to Elizabeth Prout, 1863

had no chance of recovery. In May 1863, with Father Ignatius Spencer's knowledge and the permission of Bishop Turner, she accepted the offer of a change of climate in Paris, probably with Mrs Smith, to try to improve her health. After ten days she returned, only to discover that John Smith, her great benefactor in Sutton, had been suddenly taken ill. His wife collapsed from the shock. Elizabeth nursed him until he died on 10 June 1863, nursed Mrs Smith for another fortnight and then took her to Levenshulme to recuperate.

Elizabeth was therefore in Levenshulme when she received news from Father Ignatius Spencer that Pope Pius IX had approved her Rule. Her joy was so great that her health collapsed. She made her final retreat in July 1863, under Father Salvian Nardocci, as a preparation for death. Her mission was over. The 1863 Rule was her last will and testament. In August 1863 Bishop Turner canonically established her Congregation in a ceremony in Levenshulme convent that presented a happy contrast to the investigation of

1858. At the First General Chapter on 23 October 1863 Elizabeth Prout was unanimously elected as the First Superioress General of her Congregation.

In the final months before her death, Elizabeth both experienced and demonstrated the depths of her identification with Our Lord in His Passion. In August 1863 Father Ignatius Spencer became Rector of St Anne's Monastery, Sutton. He arrived on 27 August, the anniversary of Blessed Dominic Barberi's death in 1849, as the custodian of his incorrupt body which had been brought to Sutton in 1855. As the Father of both religious houses, Father Ignatius Spencer was now more than ever in a position to help Elizabeth Prout to complete the course on which Blessed Dominic and Father Gaudentius had set her in the 1840s. She received the last rites from Father Joseph Gasparini, Vice-Rector in Sutton, in mid December 1863, evincing wonderful calm and re- collection. The Sutton annalist described how, although previously troubled about her infant Congregation, she was afterwards filled with a wonderful confidence and peace, like the peace and confidence of a child reposing on its mother's bosom in a soft slumber. Elizabeth had scaled the heights of Passionist spirituality. She had courageously accepted as God's Will what St Paul of the Cross had described as 'inner and outer fears, desolation and bodily pain'. Now she had reached the goal of resting, as he had said, 'in the bosom of the heavenly Father', ready for her exaltation with the Risen Christ. On Christmas Day she called all her community to her room. She spoke individually to each one. Then, as they stood around her, conscious that this was the last time that, as a group, they would listen to their Foundress, she gave them a parting exhortation, reminiscent of that given by St Paul of his Cross in 1775, encouraging them to perseverance in their vocation. According to religious custom in her Congregation, before they left they knelt to ask a blessing. 'God bless you, Sisters' would therefore have been her last words to her community. Then they all departed, in tears and silence.

On 3 January, the birthday of St Paul of the Cross, all the Professed Sisters made their final vows, Elizabeth Prout in

14. Fr Ignatius Spencer CP

Sutton to Father Joseph Gasparini, the rest in Levenshulme to Father Ignatius Spencer. The Congregation was now secure.

On 4 January Elizabeth sent Mother Winefride Lynch, her first consultor, to close the Ashton convent, since the sewing schools were coming to an end. The trauma of closing this work for the mill girls took its toll, for when Mother Winefride returned on 6 January, she found Elizabeth worse in health, although calm and resigned.

There still remained one important task Elizabeth Prout must perform as Foundress. Like Father Gaudentius, she had legislated for both industry and education. She had established workrooms and had set on foot the final arrangements for Homes for the mill girls. On 28 December 1863 she had received a distinguished teacher, Jane Mary Durie, into the novitiate in Sutton. In January 1864 she appointed her to take charge of St Joseph's school, Peasley Cross, with the prospect of Mother Winefride's sister as a pupil teacher. Thus Elizabeth Prout established education, including teacher training, as part of the apostolate of her Congregation.

On 9 January 1864 Father Ignatius Spencer heard Elizabeth's last confession. Very early in the morning of

11 January she was seized with violent pains. At 4 a.m. Mother Winefride was called. Every kind of application was tried but to no avail. The pains continued until four o'clock in the afternoon and all that time Elizabeth remained resigned and patient. Amongst her own community, as amongst the Passionists, she already had a reputation for sanctity, for the Sutton annalist wrote, 'It would seem from this last but severe pain that some dross still remained to be atoned for and that Our Dear Lord sent this as an atonement.' From about 5 p.m. her breathing became short but she remained perfectly conscious. When told she was dying, she gave a grateful and affectionate glance to the Sisters attending her and then she collected herself in prayer. The rest of the Sutton community came in to say the prayers for the departing and Father Ignatius Spencer was sent for. As he entered the room, she turned and recognized him with a grateful glance. It was only five minutes before her death. As she died, Father Ignatius gave her a final absolution. 'So peacefully and calmly,' wrote the Sutton annalist, 'did her soul separate from her body that we scarcely knew she was dead and her spirit had passed to her Dear Lord and Spouse. May she rest in peace.'

Father Ignatius Spencer wrote in his Diary, 'Saw Rev. Mother die at 6', his terseness hiding his grief. He wrote immediately to inform Bishop Turner. The Bishop's reply on 12 January was typical of the unwavering trust he had always had in her.

> I received your favour informing me of the death of the Rev. Mother. Well, she did a good thing in her life by establishing the Institute of the Holy Family, and I trust she is now enjoying the rewards of her labours. The Order will, I think, go on well but it is a work of time. Great progress has been made of late and I have confidence in the future.

On Tuesday, 12 January, Elizabeth's remains were laid out in the convent chapel according to the Rule, her feet bare, her body clothed in her religious habit, her modified Passionist Sign over her heart, the scroll of her vows and her crucifix in

15. Holy Cross Convent, Paradise Row, Sutton, St Helens

16. The old St Anne's Church, Sutton – interior

her hands. Word of her death was passed immediately round the Passionist houses, a clear indication of her recognized position in the Passionist family.

Her funeral took place in St Anne's church, Sutton on 14 January 1864. The coffin was carried from the convent by eight of the Professed Sisters, the rest walking in solemn procession behind. They were met by the Passionists in surplices; the celebrant, Father Leonard Fryer, since Father Ignatius Spencer had had to leave for a mission; and the acolytes, all of whom joined in the procession, chanting the Office for the Dead in a most solemn manner. A Solemn Requiem Mass was sung in the church and then Elizabeth Prout was interred in the monastery cemetery.

Chapter Eight

Reputation for Holiness

Father Gaudentius Rossi had been convinced that God had chosen Elizabeth Prout as the Foundress of his Congregation. Her care of her fever-stricken Sisters in later 1853 had led him to comment that her dispositions of mind were such that they gave him great edification and great joy to the very angels and saints of heaven. He was fully convinced of both her purity of intention and her sincere and earnest desire to advance the spiritual and temporal interests of the Holy Family. He acknowledged her humility and, in 1855, her meekness and patience. Although his mind was soured against her by those Sisters who left, and even after they left, he nevertheless admitted that they were jealous of her and that he could not believe that she had been jealous of them. Two years after her death and more than ten years since he had seen her, he remembered her many good qualities and great virtues.

Father Ignatius Spencer also held her in great esteem. He acknowledged her knowledge and abilities. He encouraged her as Foundress and Mother of her Sisters to lead them in seeking perfection. He applauded how she kept up her spirit nobly through all her difficulties, meeting them gallantly.

Father Salvian Nardocci, novice-master and a notably severe critic, had the highest regard for her. Recording the news of her death in his diary in January 1864, he wrote, 'The death of this Holy Sister will be felt very much by the Sisters. In the Reverend Mother Mary Joseph they have lost their Foundress and guide.'

Elizabeth Prout had a reputation for holiness both during her lifetime and for long after her death. Her Sisters unanimously elected her as Superior of the Congregation in 1851, 1854 and 1863. In 1872, almost ten years after her death, Father Salvian Nardocci still remembered her so well that he wrote in the Annals of the Anglo-Hibernian Province of the Passionists,

> She governed her Congregation with great skill and prudence for the space of thirteen years and many were the trials and contradictions she had to endure the whole of that time. God Almighty gave her strength to overcome them all and when the time of her dissolution came she had the consolation to see her Institute taking deep root and its branches spreading in several places.

Father Ignatius Spencer also died in 1864, on 1 October, at Carstairs in Scotland. His remains were brought back to St Anne's, Sutton and interred in the crypt near those of Blessed Dominic Barberi. The Passionist Provincial, Father Ignatius Paoli, was as keen as Father Peter Paul Cayro on the aggregation of her Congregation to the Passionist Congregation. He appointed Father Eugene Martorelli, previous Visitor General and then Provincial, as the Sisters' Director. It then fell to Father Eugene to negotiate with the authorities in Rome for both aggregation and approbation. He was supported by Father Ignatius Paoli who became a General Consultor, resident in Rome. By 1873 Elizabeth Prout's successor, Mother Winefride Lynch, had also died and had been followed as General by Mother Mary Margaret Chambers. Attracted to the Congregation by Father Ignatius Spencer and trained as a novice by the Foundress herself, she asked the Passionist Father General for permission to wear the full Passionist Sign. Her request was granted on 9 November 1874. On 15 November the new Father General, Dominic Giacchini, wrote to her,

> I have come to understand that among the pious practices and holy exercises prescribed by the Rule for the Sisters, there is

assigned a distinct place for salutary meditation on the sorrowful mysteries of the Passion of Our Divine Redeemer, joined to a special study to awaken in the hearts of others also a pious and grateful Memory of the same. The Congregation of the Sisters of the Most Holy Cross and Passion of Our Lord Jesus Christ is already in possession of the first place in my heart after that which is due to the Sons and Daughters of St Paul of the Cross.

It was more fitting than he realized that he sent her the Passionist Sign through Father Bernard O'Loughlin, 'good Father Bernard' who had played such a significant role in the 1858 investigation. Mother Mary Margaret's reply could have been Elizabeth Prout's,

No words can express the joy which your Paternity's letter and the beautiful and holy Badge of the Passion which it accompanied has brought to my heart and the hearts of all the Sisters of the Most Holy Cross and Passion. We can only offer the feeble expression simple words can convey of the imperishable gratitude in which we shall ever hold in memory the favour you have done us in assigning us our place as children of St Paul of the Cross.

It was in this context that the new chapel was opened at 31 Byrom Street, Manchester on 21 November 1874 and that on 9 April 1875, as part of the celebrations to mark the centenary of the death of St Paul of the Cross, Father Alphonsus O'Neill presented each Sister with the full Passionist Sign. Thus Elizabeth Prout's Congregation attained its true identity as part of the Passionist Congregation.

Chapter Nine

Elizabeth Prout's Founding Charism

When Elizabeth Prout died she had twenty-one Sisters in her Congregation: seven English, two American, one Scottish and eleven Irish. Within a century they and their successors had taken her apostolate to the industrial towns of Lancashire and Yorkshire, to faraway Bulgaria, to Ireland, to the Scottish mining communities of Ayrshire and Fife, to the United States, to Chile and Argentina and to the desert of Botswana. In the future they would go to Papua New Guinea, to Sweden, Peru, Jamaica, Romania, Transylvania, Bosnia-Herzegovina and Australia. In making themselves 'a holocaust of love', as Father Ignatius Spencer had expressed it, in union with the Sacrifice of Calvary, they spread their Passionist light and warmth through all these nations of the world. Thus, by co-operating with the Passionist Congregation in its mission to England and its neighbouring kingdoms, Elizabeth Prout had played a major role in extending that mission, as Father Gaudentius Rossi had wished, to the eastern and western hemispheres.

At twenty-nine years of age in 1849–50, Elizabeth Prout had been the youngest, and the first, Catholic Englishwoman to found a religious Congregation in nineteenth-century England. At great personal risk, she embraced a religious life aimed at offering the poor religious life itself. That was her primary apostolate, her radical option for the poor. It was she who first made consecrated religious life, with choir observance and no dowry for admission, available to women of the lower middle and working classes. In religious terms she put them socially on a par with the endowed orders. In spiritual terms she enabled them to reach heights of sanctity. She gave them a truly contemplative life. Her Congregation's lifestyle was not shaped by apostolic activity but by its essential 'Memory'. She gave her Sisters a way of life, a mysticism of the heart, not an intellectual or apostolic spirituality based on the will. She did not begin with concern for the poor but with the 'Memory' of the Holy Family and the Passion. It was that 'Memory', always in her heart and mind, that motivated her lifestyle and produced the kind of person who would be concerned for the distress of the poor and who would also be capable of facing the realities of Manchester's worst slums.

Her Homes for factory girls were significantly an extension of her religious Congregation. She sought to incarnate the 'Memory' of the Holy Family in the refuge. Hence it was properly called the 'Home'. Similarly, she brought that 'Memory' into the homes of the poor through her parish visitation and the children she taught. It was that emphasis on the contemplative nature of her Congregation that permitted its diversity of active apostolate. The success of the Sisters' active ministry, however, depended on the quality of their contemplative life, for, whilst other women could teach or visit the poor, only Passionists could impart their particular brand of spirituality. In contrast to the increasing permissiveness and materialism of her time, she moved towards greater austerity. Her Sisters were truly contemplatives in action. Their union with God was the dynamic force behind their active apostolate and the source from which they renewed their apostolic strength.

Her contribution to the development of Passionist spirituality was outstanding. By founding a Passionist religious Congregation specifically for lower-class women, she fulfilled to an eminent degree the teaching of St Paul of the Cross that holiness was within the reach of every human person of any class. She demonstrated that women from any class of society could receive a call from God to serve Him in consecrated religious life. Whereas St Paul of the Cross had founded the totally contemplative Passionist Nuns, Elizabeth Prout extended his apostolate by founding a female institute that accurately reflected his male Congregation in combining the contemplative and active lives.

Like St Paul of the Cross, Elizabeth did not want anything of herself to remain in her Congregation. She lived on in her Congregation, however, through the Paulacrucian spirituality which she, Father Gaudentius Rossi and Father Ignatius Spencer imparted to it; which she developed into a clearer Passionist charism in her 1863 Rule; and which, through that Rule, she invited every Sister to share in the circumstances of her own life. Her aim was a radical identification with Christ in His Passion. This austerity led her into intimate union with her Crucified Spouse, whilst also enabling her to find Him in the 'crucified' poor in Manchester's sordid slums. She and her Sisters were parish Sisters from the start.

As the Foundress of the Sisters of the Cross and Passion, Elizabeth Prout shines as the sole woman in a galaxy of eminently holy Passionists of the Anglo-Hibernian Province: Blessed Dominic Barberi, whom she knew in Stone; St Charles Houben of Mount Argus, whom she knew in Sutton; the saintly Father Ignatius Spencer, her friend and mentor; the saintly Father Paul Mary Pakenham, first Rector of Mount Argus; Father Bernard O'Loughlin, her own 'good Father Bernard', the 'saint' of Broadway; and, of course, Father Gaudentius Rossi, her co-Founder.

Conclusion

17. The Shrine of Blessed Dominic Barberi

With the permission of the Home Office, on Wednesday, 20 June 1973, a cold, wet day in north-west England, the remains of Elizabeth Prout were quietly exhumed from her grave in St Anne's cemetery, Sutton. Her bones lay covered by her religious habit, still intact, her rosary beads falling down from the leather girdle round her waist, her veil surrounding her skull. About the same time, the coffins of Blessed Dominic Barberi and Father Ignatius Spencer were also moved.

On Monday, 30 July 1973, in brilliant sunshine, after a

Mass of Thanksgiving in the old St Anne's church, where her Requiem had taken place, the remains of Elizabeth Prout and of Father Ignatius Spencer were carried in triumph to the new Church of St Anne and Blessed Dominic Barberi. There, surrounded by her daughters, the Sisters of the Cross and Passion, no longer 'sad and sorrowful' as in 1864 but singing joyfully, they were placed one on the right, the other on the left of the shrine of that other eminent Passionist and Apostle of England, their father and friend, Blessed Dominic Barberi.

Then, on 18 May 1994, the Cause for the ultimate Canonization of the Servant of God, Elizabeth Prout, was opened in St Anne's, Sutton by His Grace Archbishop Derek Worlock of Liverpool.

A Prayer for the Beatification of Elizabeth Prout

O God, source of all life, Your servant, Elizabeth Prout, responded to Your Call by bringing together a new religious family to welcome the poor and the abandoned and to keep alive the Memory of Your Love for all Your children, shown to us in the Passion of Jesus, Your Son. Give us courage to follow her example of living faith and untiring love. Through her intercession, grant us the favour for which we pray: .... Amen.

18. Elizabeth Prout's window in Bl. Dominic's Shrine

Index

Printed in the United Kingdom by
Lightning Source UK Ltd., Milton Keynes
137241UK00001B/10-189/P